SOUTER LIGHTHOUSE
and The Leas

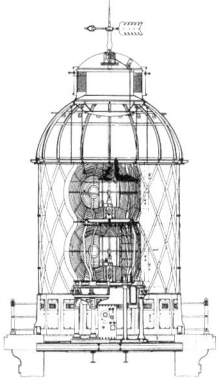

Tyne and Wear

The National Trust

A Light for the Coast

At 6.30 on the evening of 16 November 1866 the *Sovereign* from North Shields struck Marsden Rock. Her crew of eleven managed to scramble ashore, but many were not so lucky. In 1869 no fewer than 20 vessels came to grief between South Shields and Sunderland. Whitburn Steel, the stretch of submerged rocks off Whitburn and Marsden, was a particularly hazardous spot, and there were even stories of local people luring ships on to the rocks with false lights in order to plunder their cargoes.

The problem had worsened with the growth of heavy industry from Sunderland to Newcastle in the mid-nineteenth century. Coastal traffic expanded rapidly between the Tyne and the Wear, despite the arrival of the railways, as it remained cheaper to move bulk cargoes like coal and iron ore by sea. The local fishing fleet was also growing to feed the increasing population and shipping routes to Scandinavia and the Continent were opening up to export the manufactures of the North East. Heavy industry brought heavy pollution, which combined with sea fog to create a further hazard to seafarers. By the 1860s it was clear that something had to be done.

The answer was a new lighthouse at Souter, which was designed by James Douglass, Chief Engineer to Trinity House, the national lighthouse authority. At the opening in January 1871 Sir Frederick Arrow, Deputy-Master of Trinity House, 'made bold to say that no lighthouse in any part of the world would bear comparison with it'. This was no empty boast, as the Souter light was at that time one of the most technologically advanced in the world, being the first designed to be powered by electrical alternators.

Souter from the south

When Souter lighthouse was first built, it had stood alone, but it was soon surrounded by the village of Marsden, which housed those who had come to work in the nearby mine. Allotments spread along the cliff-tops, but the coastline of The Leas, and in particular the massive outcrop of Marsden Rock, remained largely untouched, a precious habitat for nesting sea-birds and coastal flora and for those simply wanting a breath of fresh air. The importance of preserving this area from development was recognised in 1987, when South Tyneside Metropolitan Borough Council gave it to the National Trust, generously underwriting the management costs for the first 50 years. The following year Trinity House decided to close down Souter Lighthouse, because of the decline in coastal shipping. The National Trust cares for places of 'historic interest' as well as 'natural beauty', and so also agreed to buy the lighthouse, which has become a focus and base for its coastal operations. Souter continued to provide aid to seamen through an automatic radio beacon until 1999, and still welcomes visitors, as it has done since 1871.

Grace Darling rescuing survivors from the wreck of the *Forfarshire* in 1838; painted by William Bell Scott, 1860 (Wallington, Northumberland). Her father was lighthouse keeper on the Farne Islands and her nephew served at Souter for 24 years

The *Alphonse* wrecked on South Beach, 28 January 1910

Douglass's Eddystone lighthouse, with the stump of the previous tower, which he dismantled

Lighthouse builders come in families. Douglass's father, Nicholas, was Super-intendent Engineer to Trinity House; his brother, William, became responsible for all the lighthouses in Ireland. He had a nomadic childhood, and by 1847 was assisting his father in building Bishop Rock lighthouse on an incredibly exposed outcrop west of the Scillies. Even with new pneu-matic tools, quick-drying cement and his floating workshop, the steamboat *Hercules*, building a rock lighthouse was still an extremely hazardous business in the mid-nineteenth century. But James Douglass was totally fearless and a man who always led from the front. In October 1859, while working on the Smalls Rock lighthouse near Milford Haven, Douglass's party were engulfed by a storm. They were given up for dead, but three days later their boat reached

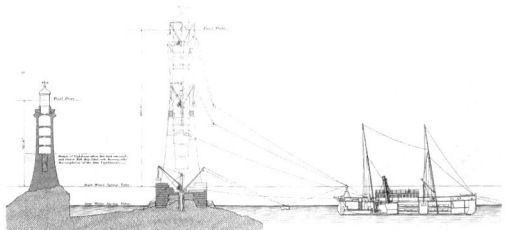
Building the Eddystone lighthouse

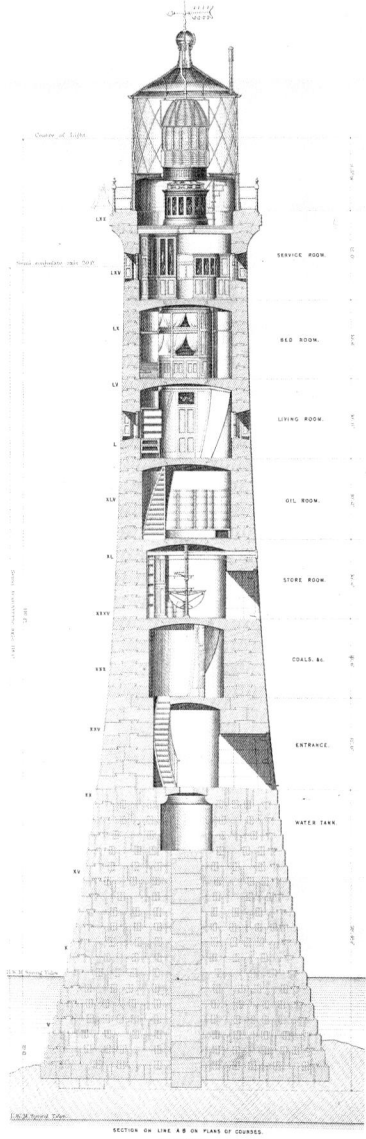

James Douglass (1826–98); lithograph by G.B. Black, 1879

the safety of Swansea harbour after an epic voyage. Douglass's son William, another lighthouse builder, was to die of exposure following a similar storm.

Even more dangerous than the Smalls was the Wolf Rock lighthouse, which Douglass erected in 1861 on a submerged reef eight miles south-west of Land's End. Battered by the full force of the open Atlantic, Douglass and his men had to be tied to the rock to avoid being swept away. Somehow they managed to construct a tower on this desolate spot, and the following year he was made Chief Engineer to Trinity House. However, the project with which his name will always be associated is the Eddystone lighthouse. Its four predecessors, which had guided sailors into Plymouth harbour, had been undermined by storm or fire. Between 1878 and 1882 Douglass created an entirely new tower from dovetailed blocks of Cornish granite. A combination of faultless engineering and elegant architecture, it has survived to this day, although since 1982 it has operated automatically. For his achievement Douglass received a knighthood in 1882. Souter gave him an important opportunity to experiment with new lighthouse technology.

The Wolf Rock lighthouse

Building Souter Lighthouse

Douglass first selected a site for his new lighthouse on Souter Point midway between the Tyne and the Wear, but by 1870 had decided to build on the higher cliffs at Lizard Point a mile further north. Away from the worst of the industrial pollution, a light here would be more visible from a shorter (and cheaper) tower. There was only one problem: Trinity House already had a Lizard Point lighthouse – in Cornwall. So to avoid confusion, the name of the original site was retained.

The tower Douglass designed stood 345 yards from the cliff edge, when first built; coastal erosion has since brought the sea much nearer. Over 75 feet high, the tower was constructed by Robert Allison of nearby Whitburn from rubble masonry, covered in Portland cement to protect it from the weather. Again in order to provide the best shelter in a gale, the other buildings were laid out on the landward side of the tower around a square courtyard with a covered inner corridor. They comprised an engine and boiler house, coke store, workshop, storeroom and dwellings for the lighthouse staff and their families. Each of the six houses had its own stone-walled front garden and backyard with wash-house, netty (outside lavatory) and fuel store. The little entrance porch opened on to the central staircase hall, which was flanked downstairs by kitchen and parlour (often doubling as the parents' bedroom) and two bedrooms upstairs. Doors connecting the adjoining houses enabled those with large families to borrow bedrooms from un-married keepers next door.

The boilers that powered the light and the foghorn needed large quantities of water, but there were no natural springs or streams on the headland, and so Douglass incorporated rainwater tanks capable of holding 60,000 gallons into the foundations of the inner courtyard and outside the Engine Room.

Souter in the late nineteenth century. The tall boiler house chimney was taken down in 1914, when the station was converted to oil. The foghorn house on the right still has its original single horn (see p. 17)

The light tower from the east

Lighting

The first lighthouses had been lit by wood or coal fires or tallow candles, and accidents were common: a chimney fire burnt down the third Eddystone lighthouse in 1775. Gas and oil lamps were developed as an alternative during the early nineteenth century, but neither proved very satisfactory. The solution was electricity. Souter was the first lighthouse in the world to be lit by Prof. Holmes's alternating current magneto-electric generator. This worked on the principle discovered by Michael Faraday that a magnet could generate an electric current in a coil of wire which passed backwards and forwards between its poles. In 1858 Holmes had begun experimenting with a generator of this kind at South Foreland lighthouse in Kent (now also in the care of the National Trust). The light itself was produced by passing electric current over a 1/16 inch gap between two 'pencils' of carbon to create a spark. The carbon lasted only four hours, so had to be regularly checked and changed. However, the results were very encouraging, as Faraday himself reported:

The light produced is powerful beyond any other that I have yet seen so applied, and in principle may be accumulated to any degree; its regularity in the lantern is great, its management easy, and its care there may be confided to attentive keepers of the ordinary degree of intellect and knowledge.

Faraday's enthusiasm was fully justified. At Souter there was an emergency oil lamp, in case the electric light failed, but in the first eight years this only happened twice – on one occasion because smoke from testing the emergency light had masked an electrical contact, and on the other because the keeper on watch had fallen asleep.

The turntable mechanism of the Souter lantern

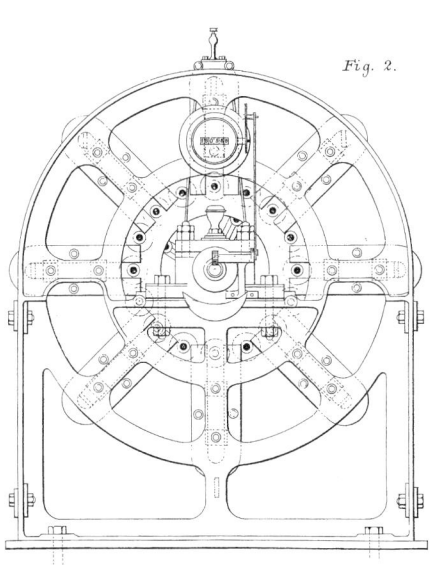

Prof. Holmes's magneto-electric generator

Fig. 2.

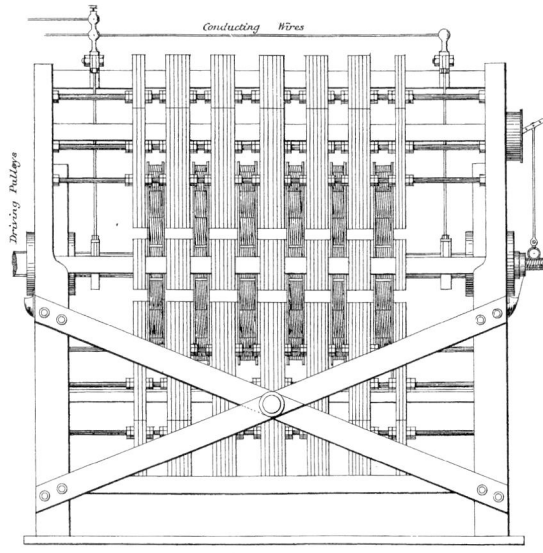

Right: Douglass's design for the Souter lantern

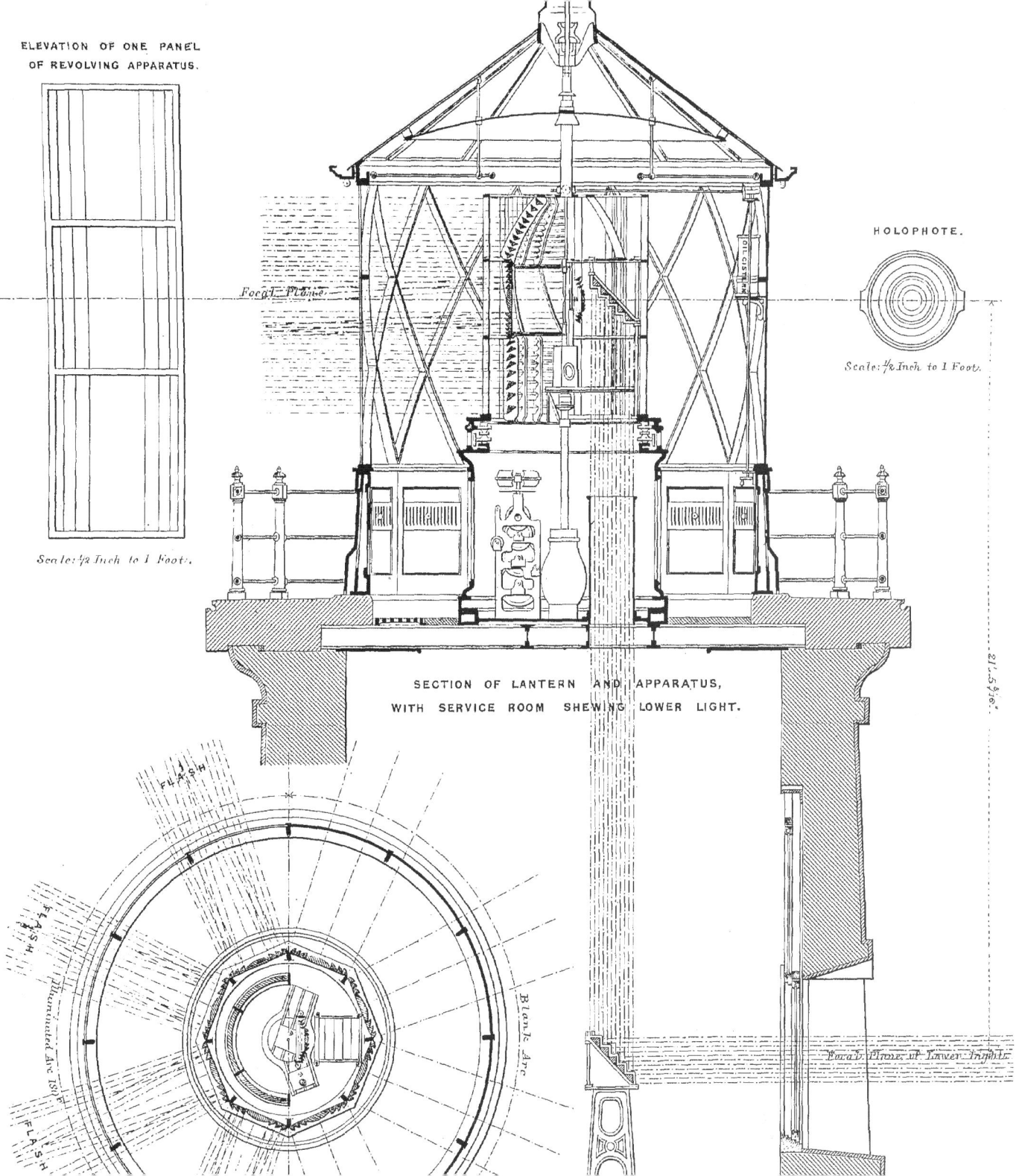

ELEVATION OF ONE PANEL
OF REVOLVING APPARATUS.

Scale: 1/2 Inch to 1 Foot.

Focal Plane.

HOLOPHOTE.

Scale: 4/2 Inch to 1 Foot.

SECTION OF LANTERN AND APPARATUS,
WITH SERVICE ROOM SHEWING LOWER LIGHT.

FLASH

FLASH

FLASH

Illuminated Arc 180°

Blank Arc

Focal Plane of Lower Lights.

Lighting

A bright, reliable light was the first require-ment; it then had to be properly focused. This was done inside the lantern by a rotating octagonal drum, each side of which consisted of seven vertical lenses that condensed and reflected the light out to sea in a series of eight distinct but adjoining beams. The battery of lenses multiplied the original light 230 times, to give it a power equivalent to 700,000 candles. From January 1871 it flashed white light for five seconds at 30-second intervals over an arc of 180°. Major Elliot, an American light-house expert who visited Souter shortly after it was built, described the result:

After leaving the Tyne at night we stood off from Souter Point to observe the light from the sea, and it certainly surpassed in brilliancy any I have ever seen, being so bright that at a distance of several miles well-defined shadows were cast upon the deck of the *Vestal*.

For the first time at Souter, Douglass provided a turntable in the lantern that extended to the full diameter of the appar-atus. This made it steadier, and also allowed the keepers to work on the inside of the apparatus while it was rotating. However, by 1914 the machinery was showing its age. A new and larger lantern was built to improve the efficiency of the light and increase its range to over 20 miles. A bigger lens was installed on a broader turntable, which weighs 4 tons in all, but rotates easily, as it rests on a bath of 1 tons of almost frictionless mercury. The basic apparatus has changed little since then.

The light was converted from electricity to oil in 1914, but in 1952 reverted to electricity again, using 4,500 watt bulbs

capable of producing a beam of 1.5 million candlepower. The turntable was rotated by a simple weight-driven clockwork motor until an electric system was installed in the 1970s. If the turntable stopped for any reason, a keeper could crank it by hand. The green metal tube extending up the tower held the weights of the original motor, which had to be wound every hour and a quarter – one of the lighthouse keepers' principal chores.

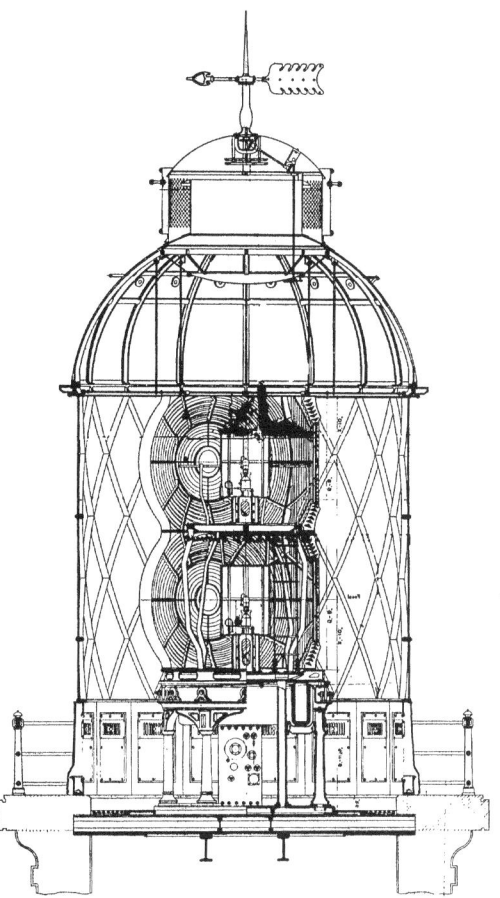

The biform lenses

The modified lantern, which was installed in 1914

Detail of one of the lenses

The Middle Light

In earlier lighthouses, half the light cast by the revolving beam was effectively wasted as it went inland. Douglass had the clever and simple idea of borrowing this wasted light to mark another hazard. By means of a series of prisms, light was reflected down 22 feet from the upper lantern and then out through another window in an arc of 31° over Sunderland Bay. And Douglass added another feature to warn seamen straying towards particularly dangerous rocks in the bay, as Major Elliot explained:

The window through which this borrowed light passes is divided vertically into parts, the one on the western or land-side being red and the other white ... When the fixed white light is seen, vessels will be in line of Mill Rock and Cape Carr Point, and when it changes to red, in that of Whitburn Stile [Steel], Hendon Rock, and White Stones.

After 1914 Douglass's innovatory system was replaced by a more conventional additional oil-burning light and lenses, apparently in order to give the keepers more to do. After 1952 it was again powered by electricity.

Map of the Durham coast, showing the hazards in Sunderland Bay illuminated by the Souter middle light; from Major Elliot's *European Light-House Systems* (1874)

The lower lantern room, showing the fixed secondary light, and (*opposite*) the spiral stairs to the upper lantern room

The Engine Room

The Engine Room is the heart of Souter, providing a reliable and instantly available source of power for the whole station. When the lighthouse was first built, it contained two of Prof. Holmes's magneto-electric generators and two Cornish boilers supplied by the Fairbairn Engineering Company, which consumed 100 tons of coke a year.

The present machinery remains just as it was when Trinity House handed over the lighthouse to the National Trust in 1990. The room is dominated by two compressors, which supplied compressed air to the foghorns outside. That on the left is electrically driven and was first installed in 1961. If for any reason it failed, then the diesel-powered compressor next to it would take over, pumping air at 60lb per square inch into the two circular storage tanks on the left, against the moment when the fog came down. Since 1952 electricity has been provided by the National Grid, but in the event of a power cut, the standby Petter diesel generator would ensure that the Souter light never went out.

What is now the shop used to be the boiler house and fuel store. The smoke was carried away by a tall, centrally placed chimneystack, which once stood beside the west range in line with the entrance drive. This was demolished and the range remodelled when oil replaced electricity in 1914.

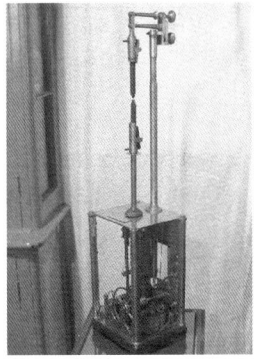

The carbon arc lamp is the mechanism that originally lit Souter's lighthouse beam. The electric current produced a flash of light as it jumped the gap between the two carbon rods. Loaned back to Souter by Sunderland Museum and Art Gallery

Frank Leaney, ex-seaman, now National Trust volunteer, cleaning the compressor

The electrically driven compressor in the foreground filled the two tanks with the compressed air needed to sound the foghorns

The Foghorns

The two black foghorns that stand on top of their own building to the east of the lighthouse tower are the successors of that provided by Prof. Holmes in 1871. The original, single horn was painted white, shaped rather like a clay pipe and faced straight out to sea. This was replaced by two similar-shaped horns, angled in the present way to project the noise up and down the coast. The foghorn house was later remodelled with a corner fireplace and elaborate glazed tiles. Two bays projected from its seaward corners to support the present trumpet-like horns. Although smaller than their predecessors, these are even more powerful.

When visibility fell below two miles in the daytime or the lights of the Tyne and Wear piers could not be made out at night, the horns let out a four-second blast every 45 seconds. The effect was ear-shattering, and in the early days the keepers were paid an extra twopence an hour 'noise money' for having to endure the din. Less fortunate were the other local residents, who until 1988 dreaded the arrival of foggy weather, which invariably meant noisy days and sleepless nights.

Souter in the early twentieth century, showing the second set of pipe-shaped foghorns

The foghorn house from the east

Life at Souter

The working staff at Souter in the early years consisted of a qualified engineer, Henry Millet, who was in overall charge, and four assistant lightkeepers. Apart from Millet, they were all in their twenties in 1871, but had already had experience at one of Trinity House's prototype electric lighthouses at Dungeness and South Foreland. For this training they received a 10 per cent bonus (the total annual wage bill in 1879 was £397 9s 2d). Their previous expertise also meant that few of the early keepers were local men; they came from as far afield as Milford Haven in Pembrokeshire, Portland in Dorset and Harwich in Essex.

By 1881 the population of Souter was larger and the place had a more domestic feeling. The census of that year recorded that Millet's household included his wife, eight children, an unmarried sister and a servant. One of the assistant keepers at that time was Grace Darling's nephew,

The mantelpiece in the children's bedroom

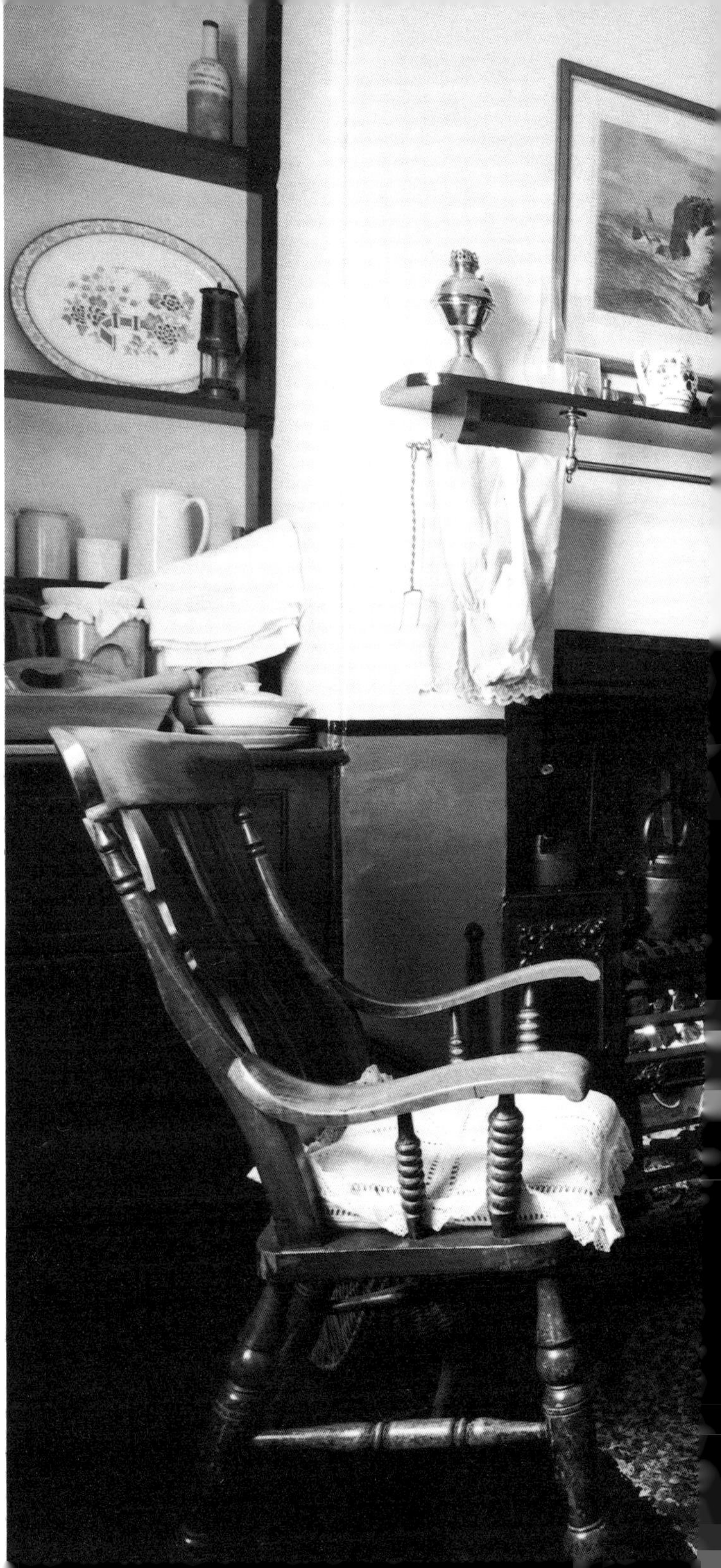

Robert, who was to work at Souter for 24 years. It was an altogether less isolated life than that on a rock lighthouse.

Douglass described the routine of the Souter keepers' day:

The watches of four hours each are kept by the four assistant keepers, one of whom is required to be constantly in the engine or boiler room, and one in the lantern, throughout the night between sunset and sunrise. Communication is established by speaking tubes between the engine room and lantern, also between the lantern and the bedroom of each lightkeeper.

Amid a myriad of mundane chores, there were occasional excitements. The keepers looked out for ships that ignored the warning lights, signalling to those that strayed too close to the rocks with flags or flares, which were kept in a cabinet on the middle light platform.

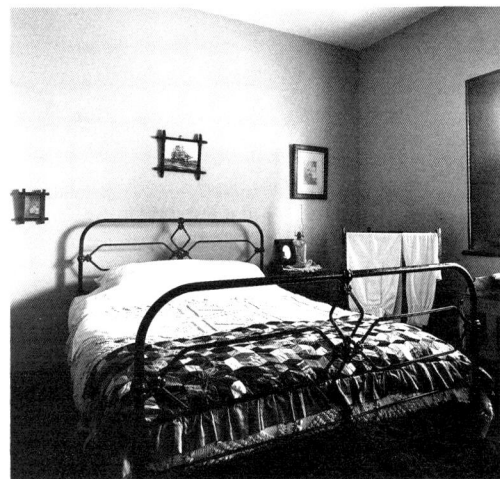

The parents' bedroom in the keeper's house

Teatime in the keeper's kitchen

The Leas

Stretching north from Souter Lighthouse are two and a half miles of magnesian limestone cliffs, wave-cut foreshore and coastal grassland, now known as The Leas. The whole of this coastline forms part of the Trow Point to Whitburn Steel Site of Special Scientific Interest. The Leas have escaped development because until the 1930s the pasture land was farmed by its owners, the Ecclesiastical Commissioners, who handed them on to the Borough Council to become an open park for the local people. The Council in turn gave The Leas to the National Trust in 1987 as part of the Trust's Enterprise Neptune campaign. Sea-birds come in increasing numbers to nest on the cliff ledges and stack tops, holidaymakers to enjoy the sandy beaches of Graham's Sands and Marsden Bay.

Marsden Bay in high summer between the wars

At the northern end of The Leas are Trow Rocks, which rise to 30 feet at Trow Point. They were once much more extensive, until quarrying began for limestone hardcore to construct the Tyne piers. An experimental 'disappearing gun' was set up on the cliff top here in 1887, when the Army was testing possible mountings for its new breech-loading coastal defence gun. A hydro-pneumatic system enabled the gun to be lowered into a concrete pit within the rock. The experiment was not a success, and the gun was removed, but has been replaced by a replica on the original foundations. South of the rocks lies a small beach known as Graham's Sands, or Ladies' Haven, after the women of Westoe village who used to bathe here.

Frenchman's Bay takes its name from a French sailing ship which ran aground here many years ago. It was once also a favourite haunt for smugglers. The next inlet is the sheltered Manhaven Bay, from which local pilots would set out when the weather in the Tyne was too rough. Here, three boathouses are set into the cliffs.

Around the headland is the broad sweep of Marsden Bay. At the north end is the small island known as Velvet Bed, which was a popular spot for picnics and bathing in the nineteenth century. Locals also call it Camel Island, because of its distinctive twin humps. Lot's Wife stands in the middle of the bay. This pillar of rock rather than salt has been created by wind and waves eroding the softer limestone strata that once encased it. Her companions, known as Jack Rock and Pompey's Wife, were formed in the same way, as were Marsden's rock arches, caves and blow-holes, and the largest and most famous stack in the bay, Marsden Rock.

County Durham fishwives in the nineteenth century

The Leas, looking north from Souter, over
Marsden Rock (before it collapsed in 1996)
and Bay, to South Shields and the mouth of
the Tyne beyond

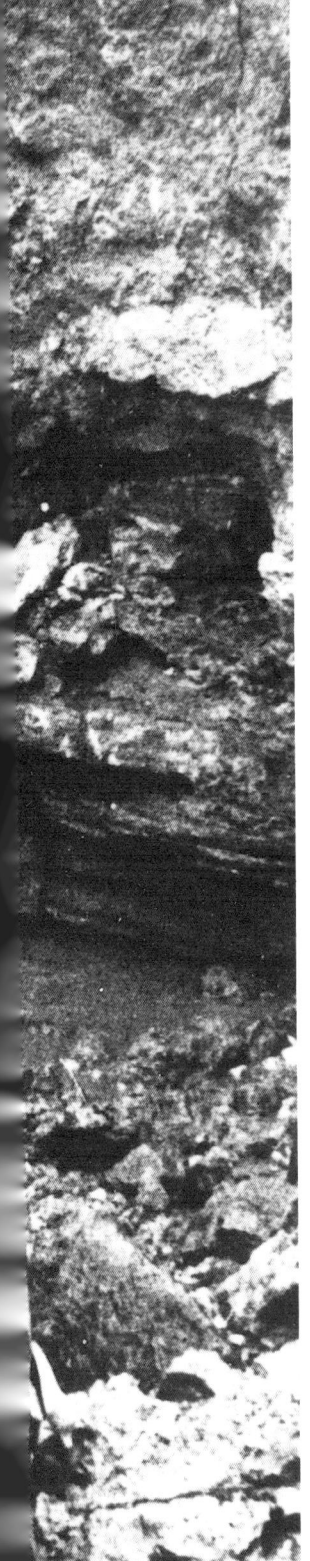

Marsden Rock

Over thousands of years since the last Ice Age Marsden Rock has become separated from the mainland by relentless erosion. Erosion has also gouged out the ledges on its 100-foot-high limestone cliffs, which provide ideal nesting places for sea-birds. As industrial development has spread along the North-East coast, the importance of Marsden Bay has grown. It is now home to the largest mainland breeding colony of sea-birds between the Tweed and the Tees – indeed is second in the region only to the Farne Islands, which are also cared for by the National Trust.

Marsden Grotto lies at the foot of the cliffs directly opposite Marsden Rock. This naturally created cave became a favourite haunt of the smugglers who worked along this stretch of coast. The grotto's first permanent occupant was 'Jack the Blaster', who set up home with his wife here in 1782. As his nickname suggests, he is said to have enlarged the cave with explosives, and probably also made the steps which climb the cliffs to the north. From his grotto home he dispensed refreshments to smugglers and to the growing number of more public visitors to the bay. He was succeeded in 1828 by Peter Allan, who excavated a ballroom out of the rock and continued the tradition of hospitality by creating a hotel here. After Allan's death his wife carried on the business, which was in turn taken on in 1874 by Sidney Milnes Hawkes. A supporter of Italian unification, he made Marsden an unlikely meeting place for his political friends.

In 1898 the brewers Vaux & Sons took over the lease of the hotel and in 1938 acquired the property outright, modernising the buildings and installing the electric lift to the cliff-top. Marsden Grotto remains in private ownership as a restaurant and public house.

Marsden Grotto in the nineteenth century

Target Rock claims another victim,
on 25 November 1925

Marsden Rock

Birds and Plants of the Coast

Only in fairly recent years have the limestone cliffs and rock stacks of Marsden Bay been colonised by sea-birds in large numbers. Kittiwakes were first found nesting on the east side of Marsden Rock in the early 1930s. Their numbers grew steadily, particularly during the Second World War, when the beach was closed to human visitors, and Marsden is now home to up to 5,250 pairs. There are also over a hundred breeding pairs of the larger fulmar, which can often be seen soaring in the up draughts from the cliff faces.

Kittiwake

Cormorants need bigger nests, which they make on the top of Marsden Rock and the nearby Pompey's Wife stack. The Marsden colony is especially important, constituting over 10 per cent of the entire English coastal breeding population. Shags and razorbills arrive in spring, and the latter were recorded breeding here for the first time in 1988. In the winter divers and guillemots hunt for fish off the coast, while turnstones and purple sandpipers can be found along the rocky shore. Lizard Point is an excellent point from which to watch the passage of migrating sea-birds in spring and autumn. In October fieldfares and redwings gather in large flocks after their long sea crossing from Scandinavia.

Maritime plants such as thrift, scurvy grass and sea plantain abound. Other species include cowslips, primroses, early purple orchid, burnet saxifrage, rockrose and harebells. For some plants like torgrass, yellow wort and bee orchid Marsden represents the northernmost point at which they will grow in Britain. Where the underlying rocks come close to the surface, they support the rich flora characteristic of magnesian limestone landscapes. One such area is opposite the disused limekilns, between the cliffs and the coastal road. Here you will find dropwort, pyramidal orchid, wild thyme, autumn gentian, small scabious, hoary plantain, kidney vetch and quaking grass. Visitors are asked not to pick the wild flowers or disturb nesting birds.

Shag

Guillemot

Thrift

Razorbill

Whitburn Colliery and Marsden

Today Souter Lighthouse is surrounded by open grass, but until recently it looked very different. Much of the best coal in the North East is to be found in strata extending out under the North Sea. The right to mine here was bought in 1873 by the Whitburn Coal Company, which began sinking two shafts south of the lighthouse the following year. However, due to water seepage, the shafts were not completed for nineteen months, and the first coal not brought out until late 1881.

Marsden village was built north of the lighthouse by Whitburn Colliery to house its miners and their families. It consisted of nine terraces of simple, mainly two-up, two-down houses; those without their own garden were given an allotment on the cliff edge to the north-east of the lighthouse. Life centred on the coal-fired range in the downstairs parlour, where miners would have to wash in a tin bath after their shift, before the colliery put in pit-head baths. The parents usually slept in the back sitting-room, their children in the upstairs bed-rooms. In the 1920s and '30s horse-drawn carts brought round meat, fish and fruit, and Mr Millet sold ice-cream from a barrow. Other supplies came from the Co-op across the main road. NUM meetings were held in the Union Room in James Street, which also served as barber's shop and for gospel meetings. The children went to the Sunday school behind Hilton Street, and, during the rest of the week, to Marsden County School, with its large sports ground, which stood south of the lighthouse until the 1930s. The Miners' Reading Room and Institute on Charles Street provided a good library downstairs and billiard tables on the floor above.

Old Marsden Inn in Lizard Lane, *c.*1950

Mining at Souter was never easy and the colliery finally closed in 1968. With the colliery gone, the village lost its purpose and has also been swept away. Broken bricks beneath the grass are all that is left of a community that lived here for almost 100 years.

The old workings have now been returned to nature as the Whitburn Coastal Park. This reclaimed area, now managed by the National Trust, includes newly planted trees, a bird observatory and wetland habitats for ducks and other creatures. It was designated a Local Nature Reserve in 2003.

Whitburn Colliery in the 1930s

Empire Day at Marsden school in the 1920s

Marsden Limekilns and Quarries

Limestone has been quarried at Marsden since the early nineteenth century, but the limekilns were not built until the 1870s, when the colliery provided a convenient local source of fuel. They were designed to burn limestone to make quick or unslaked lime (calcium oxide). This has many uses. It is added to cement to make building mortar. It is also important for the steel and chemical industries, which formed a central part of the industrial development of the North East in the nineteenth century. In its slaked form, it has traditionally been spread on the fields as a soil fertiliser.

There are two main types of limekilns to be seen at Marsden. Seven complete examples of the first version survive within a long stone battery. At the north end is an unfinished kiln, which reveals the interior lined with firebricks. The later kilns are at the south end of the battery. These are circular, and built of bricks reinforced with iron bands. Both types operated in the same way, in essence like a simple vertical oven. Alternate layers of limestone and coal were poured into the top of the kiln from railway wagons known as 'dans' or 'kibbles'. The coal was lit from the base and then left to burn slowly for about twelve hours. The immense heat generated produced quick lime, which was drawn off through the arched openings at the bottom on to the brick and concrete platform below, from which it was loaded directly into railway trucks. This was a virtually continuous process: as quick lime and clinker were removed at the bottom, more fresh materials could be added at the top.

Marsden limestone quarry around 1892

Whitburn limekilns

The Marsden Railway

In the 1870s a standard gauge railway line was built by the Harton Coal Company to link Whitburn Colliery, Marsden Quarry and the limekilns to the wider rail network at Westoe. It brought miners and supplies to the colliery and carried away coal to South Shields. Between 1885 and 1953 the railway also operated passenger services up and down the coast, doing a brisk trade in the summer with daytrippers to the beaches. The rolling stock was always fairly elderly, which earned it the nickname 'the Marsden Rattler'. In 1926 the line was moved 100 yards inland to make way for a new coastal road, and Marsden station – the smallest in England – was demolished. The coming of the road threatened the future of the line; when the colliery closed in 1968, it was the last straw. The track was taken up and the area reclaimed as public open space in the mid-1970s.

The Marsden railway line once ran west of Souter

Miners at Whitburn Colliery in 1954

The Marsden railway was built to serve
Whitburn colliery